Contents

||| | |||||| || | ||||| || ||| ||| |||
I0164484

Articles on
The Writings of St. Augustine

(St Augustine of Hippo 354-430)

By Colin Smith

ISBN: 978 1 78364 625 8

www.obt.org.uk

Introduction

Introduction

Every so often when I am reading, a phrase or short sentence grabs my attention and raises my curiosity. It may simply be that it seems a particularly appropriate way of saying something with which I am already comfortable and accept. But occasionally it expresses something new and intriguing. So, I make a note to think about it when time permits.

The New Testament has a very large number of such short sentences, many attributed to Jesus himself. Yet it's not only the New Testament, for there is also much succinct and apt wisdom in the Old Testament. The book of Proverbs, for example was written largely with the intention of making the readers think about their behaviour, thereby stimulating, encouraging and challenging patterns of behaviour. There are still more elsewhere which are well worth "digging" for.

Challenging statements also occur naturally in everyday conversation. I remember quite a few occasions when I have been brought up sharp, and forced to reconsider my own presuppositions, by something which has been said "off the cuff", usually, but not exclusively, by a fellow believer. In fact, some people seem to have a gift for making such statements, which should be welcomed. Thinking about them can be very helpful. In fact, it has been said that such statements are one way in which God "speaks" to us personally.

In this series, I will consider a selection of such statements and comment on them. I ask you to think about them yourself, and see if you agree with me. I find many of the sayings of St Augustine of Hippo, who lived from 354 to 430 AD particularly apt, and so they are all from his writings. He would not, of course, have seen Jesus or anyone who was a direct witness of His life and teaching. However, the 27 books of the New Testament were first affirmed at the Synod of Carthage as canonical in 397AD, during Augustine's lifetime, though they would have been in circulation for a long period before that, and he would have been familiar with them.

Interestingly, he is the patron of brewers because of his conversion from a former life of loose living, which included parties, entertainment, and worldly ambitions. Consequently, his complete turnaround and conversion has been an inspiration to many who struggle with a particular vice or habit, which they long to break. He was also highly educated for his time, and wrote several books which remain important to philosophers and theologians today. Many of his writings have survived. Here are two quotes worth thinking about.

> i) Oh Lord, give me chastity, but do not give it yet,

and

> ii) If you believe what you like in the gospels, and reject what you don't like, it is not the gospel you believe, but yourself.

I will give you my thoughts on them in a later article, but what are yours?

Oh Lord, give me chastity, but do not give it yet.

St. Augustine: Article 1

Oh Lord, give me chastity, but do not give it yet.

St Augustine of Hippo strongly influenced the development of Christianity. Today, he is still seen as one of the most important of the early Church Fathers.

This quotation from one of his surviving books suggests that, at least in his young days, he was a bit of a lad - and indeed he was. He had to abandon his concubine, who he loved, in favour of a lady who his mother arranged for him to marry. This entailed a two year wait until his fiancée came of age.

During that time. he confessed to being a slave to lust - whilst also being a thoughtful and sincere believer. So. he cried out in anguish for the help of God in overcoming this sin.

I am sure that many believers today similarly cry out, in the same way. And many find help in the very realistic words of St Paul to the Romans.

> For the good that I would I do not: but the evil which I would not, that I do. (Romans 7:19 KJV)

It seems that St Paul was having a similar difficulty. I take comfort in the fact that most believers today also share this kind of struggle. Knowing this, eases my own anguish, but without condoning the sin.

The reasons for the inner conflict, however, needs a bit more thinking about. For example, why is it that we continue to sin even when we genuinely wish to do better?

These and similar questions drove me to Article the rest of Romans to try to make sense of my experience. The outcome is related to our understanding of humankind both before and after coming to faith. A fuller explanation is however better left for another time, and another place. But, for now, there is another important point to be considered.

Are we not seeing Paul's teaching in the verse above, through the eyes of our 21st Century Western society? Indeed, many commentators see an obsession with sex as pervading our current culture.

But read Romans 7:19 again. There is no mention of sexual sin there. He seems to be making a general point about the evil within, rather than about specific sins related to sexual behaviour.

So, this verse can equally well relate to the sins of pride, gluttony, greed, and covetousness. Or indeed any habitual sin.

Even if we have never involved ourselves with fornication, adultery, incest or prostitution, who amongst us can claim to be free of all other sins? And who amongst us has not felt the anguish of letting down our Lord once again?

Praise Him that his forgiveness is freely given. However, don't take this as an excuse for licentiousness! Instead prayerfully lay your problems before him, and await his response.

You will not be disappointed.

If you believe what you like
in the gospels,
and reject what you
don't like,
it is not the gospel you
believe,
but yourself.

St. Augustine: Article 2

If you believe what you like in the gospels, and reject what you don't like, it is not the gospel you believe, but yourself.

So here we go again! Not only did St. Augustine want to carry on sinning until some indeterminate time in the future, as we saw in the last article, but also, he wanted everyone to believe everything in the gospels.

This would not have gone down well with the theologians and church leaders of his day. Nor would it go down well today for we value our freedoms, especially our right to our own opinion and beliefs.

St. Augustine certainly had a knack for provoking thought by making challenging statements. Had he lived in earlier times he would probably have been seen as a prophet. Today he would more likely be deemed "awkward", and ignored. But what is he actually saying? And is it helpful?

Let us first admit that there are plenty of challenging statements in the gospels and, remember that our faith is never just about **agreeing with** them as a set of propositions, many challenge our behaviour and thought life too.

This is hard and tricky work that may require a significant part of our valued time. Tricky because, the statements are often counter cultural. That is, they go against what is generally believed.

The temptation is to brush aside the challenges as irrelevant or self-evidently untrue, because "everyone" disagrees with them. We are effectively choosing on the basis of our culture, which we have unquestionably accepted. Or as St. Augustine puts it, we are believing only that which is accepted by those around us; i.e. ourselves.

So how do we decide what to throw out and what to keep? Ultimately, we can't. The gospels tell us everything we know about Jesus and they have been through a rigorous process of scrutiny by both the church and the apostles. So much so that they were soon accepted as being Scripture, where every "bit" is important and included for a purpose.

Augustine pointed out that we need a different attitude and need to reject the notion that we can pick and choose on the basis of our own, or our cultural, preferences. Instead, we should face the challenges and struggle with their meaning.

Other parts of the Bible, as well as Christian friends and trusted commentators, help us enormously in this. These struggles get us nearer to the truth, and we often find that we are not only searching the Scriptures, but they are searching us. And that leads to our growing in the faith.

As St Paul puts it in his second letter to Timothy 3:16:

"All Scripture is God-breathed and is useful for teaching, rebuking, correcting and training in righteousness."
(NIV)

Seek not to understand
that you may believe,
but believe
that you may understand

St. Augustine: Article 3

Seek not to understand that you may believe, but believe that you may understand.

Doesn't sound quite right does it? Accept this set of beliefs now, even though you have little idea about what they are, or what they involve, or what evidence underpins them. And don't worry for all will become clear at some time in the future!

There was a time ages ago now, when I would have completely rejected this approach as being intellectually dishonest. How can you be expected to "just believe" when there seems to be little, if any, supporting evidence. Or where different believers disagree on what the necessary beliefs are.

So, what has changed? And was this really what St Augustine meant? Two things have changed in my thinking about this statement. First my understanding of what kind of thing Christianity is, and secondly, the realisation that it is essentially revelational rather than scientific.

Christianity is not primarily a set of beliefs at all, although beliefs are involved. It's much more about being in a relationship with someone you love. Thus, exploring Christianity has little to do with collecting hard evidence, and building a theory. It is more about looking at what is on offer, and then seeing if it is sufficiently attractive, to take the plunge of entering a relationship and exploring further. The beliefs follow on from there. It's more like a courtship than a scientific investigation.

But what is involved in courting God with a view to entering a relationship? A good start would be to find out as much as possible about him or her. This can seem difficult as God has no physical form, so cannot be physically touched, seen or heard. But that is not the end of the matter, for the claim is that historically he was physically amongst us, as a man called Jesus.

To evaluate this claim, we could look at the eye witness accounts, as found in the gospels and letters of the New Testament, which the early church went to a great deal of trouble to ensure were accurate. Another useful move would be to seek the company of those who claim to know him spiritually and talk with them about their experience. In this way a picture can be gradually built up.

At this point, a tentative prayer asking Him to reveal himself might well be appropriate. Effectively he is being held to his promises such as this one:

> "Ask and it will be given to you; seek and you will find; knock and the door will be opened to you. For everyone who asks receives; he who seeks finds; and to him who knocks, the door will be opened". (Matthew 7:7-8)

It's certainly worth a try. It worked for me, the door did open as it has done for many others.

Miracles are not contrary to nature, but only contrary to what we know about nature.

St. Augustine: Article 4

Miracles are not contrary to nature, but only contrary to what we know about nature.

The importance of rational thought, based on observation, underpins all science and technology. But it was not until the Enlightenment, beginning in the late 17th Century, that it became dominant in Western society. This led to widespread scepticism about all religion. Christianity, based as it is, on the core belief in the miracle of the resurrection of Jesus, is no exception.

Yet here, in Augustine, we find a philosopher/theologian defending the reality of miracles, well over a thousand years before the Enlightenment began. It should therefore be no surprise that we still have to defend this aspect of Christianity, a mere few centuries afterwards.

One hundred years or so ago, physicists thought they were pretty close to an understanding of everything, and all that there was left to find out was a clearing up operation, dotting the i's and crossing the t's. But then along came wave-particle duality, Heisenberg's uncertainty principle, quantum theory and much more, all based on complex mathematics of mainly a statistical nature.

The particular branch of statistics most useful was probability theory. So, the mechanistic universe operating according to fixed laws of nature, was no longer a sufficient basis for understanding of the world in which we live. And there is still little sign that a "Theory of Everything" is close to being formulated.

Miracles, in the sense of events outside the laws of nature, now look more feasible, and so St Augustine's statement above is vindicated. That is, he was right in pointing out the ongoing limitations of our knowledge of the natural world.

I have found it helpful in understanding miracles, to consider them as signs pointing us towards something. The important question then is "What does it signify?" rather than "Did it really happen?" For example, following the miracle of water being changed into wine at a wedding in Cana, John records in his Gospel, Chapter 2 verse 11:

> What Jesus did here in Cana of Galilee was the first of the signs through which he revealed his glory; and his disciples believed in him.

The claim is that miraculous events occurred for a purpose. So, seek out the why, and leave the how to God.

Now Jesus did many other **signs** in the presence of the disciples,
which are not written in this book;
but these are written **so that** you may believe
that Jesus is the Christ, the Son of God,
and that by believing you may have life in his name.
(John 20:30-31)

---

i) God loves each of us as if there were only one of us.

ii) He who created us without our help will not save us without our consent.

St. Augustine: Article 5

i) God loves each of us as if there were only one of us.
ii) He who created us without our help will not save us without our consent.

The love of God is both broad and deep. We glimpse it in creation, where its beauty points us to his love After all, how can a positive outcome of any creative activity lead to anything but a love for the object created?

Yet when we consider the natural disasters that occur far too regularly we soon realise that, as we see it now, God's creation is not as it should be, according to his intentions. This applies just as much to humankind, for far from being always kind and loving, we are endemically self-centred.

This is the basis of the Christian claim, namely such is the depth and breadth of his love, that he made various attempts to put things right, which culminated in his entering His creation himself in human form, as Jesus, to offer forgiveness and life eternal to us all.

This is best expressed in the most loved and most widely translated verse in the Bible namely John 3:16.

> For God so loved the world that he gave his one and only Son, that whoever believes in him shall not perish but have eternal life.

The words of St Augustine in (i) above are more to do with magnifying God's love than elevating our own worth, so let us simply be thankful for Jesus who humbled Himself and came to earth to live and die for each of us.

What then of the second quotation in (ii) above? There is good news here too namely that God loves us so much that he will not force himself upon us. His love is not like that of a rapist (or stalker), who forces himself onto people, seeing them as little more than objects to satisfy his own desire.

We are not compelled to accept God's advances. He is offering his love to all, but like all gifts, we can refuse or ignore them. Only when we accept them gratefully and determine to live in the light of them can we be truly saved.

This leaves us with the dilemma of what happens to those who do not take up the offer, and those who have not heard of it? The answer divides Christians. Those of a liberal perspective believe that Gods love is so great that they will be saved anyway (universalism). The conservative evangelicals, on the other hand, believe that universalism is incompatible with the need for consent. That is to save everyone irrespective of an accepting response (i.e. consent) is tantamount to his forcing himself onto them for his own satisfaction. What kind of love is that?

As for me, I lean towards the evangelical view, but concentrate on living my life in relationship with God irrespective of this. Surely that is what matters most.

Charity

is no substitute

for justice withheld.

St. Augustine: Article 6

Charity is no substitute for justice withheld.

In general, we are all very happy that God has immense love for the whole of his creation, and with the call to emulate Him. This is especially so in His love for all of humankind. Thus, charity, defined as "the voluntary giving of help" out of love, is widely accepted as a joyful duty. But what then of God's justice, and its relationship to charity?

Justice may be defined as the fair and   reasonable treatment of people within their particular place in the world. Thus, justice should work to rectify those situations that give some people an excess of resources. It should seek to create a world where all have enough.

The problem with charity and justice is that too often charity is demeaning to the receiver and gives the donor unwarranted feelings of superiority. Hence it generally does little to promote justice.

When St. Augustine said, "Charity is no substitute for justice withheld" he was pointing out this problem, and implying that charity, even on a large scale, can get in the way of justice, by allowing those in power to wipe their hands of the underlying causes of poverty. Thus, in many situations, justice requires the decision to be taken out of the hands of the powerful, to ensure that everyone is provided with basic rights, and material well-being.

He is not, however, saying that good cannot be accomplished by individuals carrying out charitable acts out of conviction and compassion. Merely that most individual acts of kindness, on their own, don't help solve the underlying problem. In so doing he is echoing the words of many of the Old Testament prophets. God's anger at exploitation and greed is palpable here for example.

"The Lord enters into judgment against the elders and leaders of his people: it is you who have ruined my vineyard; the plunder from the poor is in your houses. What do you mean by crushing my people and grinding the faces of the poor?" (Isaiah 3:14,15)

And many commentators today have made the same point.

> "Overcoming poverty is not a gesture of charity.
> It is an act of justice."
> (Nelson Mandela)

> "I sit on a man's back, choking him and making him carry me, and yet assure myself and others that I am very sorry for him and wish to ease his lot by all possible means—except by getting off his back."
> (Leo Tolstoy.)

So let us, by all means, give to charity, but let us also work for the reform of unjust systems

If we did not have rational souls, we would not be able to believe.

St. Augustine: Article 7

If we did not have rational souls, we would not be able to believe.

What an intriguing statement! Most Christians are familiar with St Paul's advice to the Corinthians (2 Corinthians 5:7), to walk by faith not by sight. This seems to play down the role of rationality by equating it to walking by sight.

Yet here we have one of the early church fathers saying that our very belief is dependent on rationality. So, what is going on here? Is there really a conflict between rationality and belief? And if not, what is St Paul saying?

As with many such puzzles, the confusion arises from our understanding of the words used. Rationality may be defined as the habit of acting by reason, in accordance with observable facts. In other words, the application of valid thought processes (usually logical ones) to the facts before us.

The alternative is responding according to our emotions (i.e. what we feel, rather than what we think), but this doesn't add up to a reliable strategy for decision making. The problem is that our emotions are strongly influenced by our stress levels and our state of mind at the time.

But what of faith and belief? How do these relate to rationality? Most Christians will readily admit that Christianity is not primarily a set of statements to be accepted, or a moral code to live by. Rather it is being in a loving relationship with a living person namely Jesus the Christ, as a result of surrendering to Him, and living in the light of the consequences.

Yet this cannot come about without "weighing up" the relevant facts of history, especially that he actually existed as a human being and that he is still very much alive, having risen from being dead and is able to be in our lives today.

Thus, some rationality is needed before belief can occur. But please note that this doesn't mean that *all* the facts need to be re-examined in detail, any more than we need to understand aerodynamics before embarking on an air journey. To make a decision, to believe, is enough. Whether this decision comes about suddenly or gradually also doesn't really matter.

This is surely what St Augustine was getting at. He was thinking about the process of coming to faith, whereas St Paul is more concerned with how we live afterwards. And the role of emotions is that they are simply valuable means of expressing love, admiration, anger etc., as encouraged by the gospels. Their role in decision making is however questionable. They best come into play after the decision has been made and action is needed.

Do you agree?

Pray as though everything depended on God.

Work as though everything depended on you.

St. Augustine: Article 8

Pray as though everything depended on God. Work as though everything depended on you.

Whilst the relationship between prayer and work is not explicitly mentioned or explored in the Bible, this saying of St. Augustine is a great philosophy which many Christians have adopted and live by. When they can do nothing else, they can at least pray, or, as I once heard said, it is actually not the least they can do but the most. In prayer God is brought into the situation.

This exhortation to pray needs no specific Biblical justification, for prayer pervaded the lives of the people of that time. And many of them understood it as trying to be close to God by living in harmony with him, as many of today's Christians also do. Let us not, therefore, get too caught up with prayer as asking for things, but instead concentrate on the living in harmony aspect.

Then asking prayers become a natural consequence of that relationship. Otherwise prayer becomes yet another hard and difficult task, for us to do to please him, which is not God's intention at all.

But where does work come in? The above paragraph hints that prayer is particularly hard work if we see it *other than as* a result of being close to God. Another (later) great saint of the church, St Benedict, proclaimed that prayer is work (*ora et labora*). Whilst this is a different understanding of prayer, it does remind us that we need to work at it.

He realistically recognises that our self-centredness is a factor, in that we are often distracted by thoughts related to our situation at the time. So much so that we need to ask for the help of the Holy Spirit in operating from within our relationship with God, rather than give up because it seems to be hard work.

But this is not the end of the matter. As we seek him, he works in dialogue with us, respecting both our dignity and personal freedom. Thus, he does not normally intervene in our affairs until asked to do so, and any help that he gives will not override the will of either those praying or those prayed for. When he does intervene, he will *normally* act in such a way as to preserve stability and order in his creation rather than acting miraculously. Operating in this way, prayer can indeed be said to be the doing of his work.

God's main way of working in the world is through his people who act as channels of his love. As we pray into a situation, he needs someone to carry out his will within and around it; i.e. to work with him. In this sense also, prayer and work go together, and we should work as if the results of our prayer depend on us, for they may well do!

It is not the punishment but *the cause* that makes *the martyr.*

St. Augustine: Article 9

It is not the punishment but *the cause* that makes *the martyr.*

(St Augustine)

**It is *the cause*, not the death, that makes *the martyr.*
(Napoleon Bonaparte)**

**I'm fighting so I can die *a martyr* and go to heaven to meet God.
Our fight now is against the Americans.
(Osama bin Laden)**

**Aunty Gladys is *a martyr* to her bunions.
(Colin Smith)**

OK the last one is a bit of a joke, but none-the-less they all illustrate at least two important points.

First that the same sentiment has been used by different people in vastly different times. Secondly, they illustrate very well how the same word, martyr, changes its meaning according to the context.

"Martyr" clearly has different meanings for Colin Smith and Osama bin Laden than for St Augustine and Napoleon. Indeed, it is the underlying meaning that matters, rather than who said it. And the underlying meaning rests on our understanding of what a martyr actually is. St Augustine himself expanded on the quote above from in his writings as follows.

> There are also some among the heretics who flatter themselves with claims of martyrdom. But not all who submit their bodies to suffering, even to flames, are to be considered as having shed their blood for their sheep; rather, they may have shed it *against* the salvation of their sheep, for the Apostle says: "If I should deliver my body to be burned, and have not charity, it profits me nothing." (1 Corinthians 13:3)

On this basis Aunty Gladys is most definitely *not* a martyr as she has not submitted her body to suffering for the benefit of others. Nor is Osama bin Laden, for the kind of death he had in mind has nothing to do with either salvation or with charity.

I am not sure about Napoleon Bonaparte, but I suspect not, for his army would not have been entirely composed of willing volunteers. Furthermore, they were fighting for the conquest of lands and peoples. Not much charity involved there.

Few of us are likely to experience martyrdom but let us honour and revere our modern-day martyrs rather than cheapen their actions by using the term loosely for any kind of underserved suffering. There is much to be learnt from their lives. I particularly identify with Archbishop Luwum of Uganda and Pastor Martin Niemoller of Germany. You?

St Augustine

and the pear tree

St Augustine and the pear tree

One of my memories of my youth, was when our "gang" went door knocking on dark winters night's. It was great fun, until one night ... I got caught and was marched off back home and handed over to my Dad who "dealt with" the matter. The others ran faster than me and got away.

I now look back in mild amusement, at our childhood antics. Why is this important though? Well St Augustine as a young lad, with a few friends, did something similar by scrumping pears from a neighbours tree and feeding them to his pigs.

As the older and wiser bishop of Hippo, St Augustine looked back on his antics with a critical eye and published his thoughts in his book "Confessions" (*Confessions*, II.vi.12). It transpires that when his gang ate the pears they weren't very good and so the pigs had a bit of a feast. However, he wasn't so much concerned with the stealing the pears as with what was happening inwardly. He tried to find a motive for the crime and in a key sentence says.

"Perhaps we ate some of them, but our real pleasure consisted in doing something that was forbidden."

Thus he acknowledged that the theft was *not* prompted by need, or coercion, or by anything other than a perverse love of sin.

He confesses, *"The evil in me was foul, but I loved it."* The point being was that each pear was stolen not to be eaten, but just because of the enjoyment he got from stealing it. He didn't however, wallow in shame and self-loathing. Rather it lit a fire within him which became a restlessness that drove him close to God. This led him to seek greater perfection, whilst acknowledging that all humans need divine grace if they are to reach an inner peace.

Ever since then philosophers, theologians and psychologists have looked back with interest on St Augustine's thoughts. For me, he is right in identifying the evil within us (sometimes spoken of as "original sin"). Moreover, he goes further, and points out that often we enjoy the sin, and realises that this leads to distress and unease. Sadly some Christians appear to continuously struggle and strive to overcome this evil within, rather than use prayer and reflection to bring a simple acceptance of Gods good and gracious gifts.

Have you tried this approach?

What does

love look like?

What does love look like?

It has the hands to help others.
It has the feet to hasten to the poor and needy.
It has eyes to see misery and want.
It has the ears to hear
the sighs and sorrows of men.
That is what love looks like.

We have the same word for falling snow, packed snow, slushy snow, driven snow and many other forms of snow. To most of us it is simply "snow".

However, for the Eskimo/Inuit people this would seem very strange indeed. It is self-evident to them that there is more than one type of snow, important enough to need different words to identify them (some estimates give 50).

Similarly, in Jesus' time it was self-evident to people that there was more than one type of love, each significantly different and therefore needing different words.

In researching this piece, I found there were four words for love. It is instructive to briefly consider each in turn.

Eros relates to sensual, romantic love often characterised by physical attraction, and involving a strong emotional bond.

Philia is also characterised by an emotional bond, based on shared interests particularly for siblings and close family. Thus, it is sometimes referred to as brotherly love, but can also be applied to close friendships with non-family members.

Storge is an interesting one, and similar to philia except that it is used only for family members and is referred to simply as family love.

Agape is by far the most important form of love which Christians think of as divine love. It differs from the others in that it is unconditional and available for all. Furthermore, it is not based on personal circumstances or feelings but, is founded upon actions. Feelings may accompany the actions, but receiving or giving it has no expectation of anything in return. It is essentially love in action.

Agape love is how God loves each and every one of us and it is how He wants us to love one another. It is the kind of love that St Augustine describes in the quote above. It is sacrificial and is demonstrated most powerfully in the willingness of Jesus to endure suffering and death because of it. No less may be required of us.

There is no greater love than to lay down one's life for one's friends.
(John 15:13)

I have read in Plato and Cicero

St. Augustine: Article 12

I have read in Plato and Cicero

sayings that are wise and very beautiful; but I have never read in either of them: "Come unto me all ye that labour and are heavy laden."

This quotation invites the questions "Who on earth are Plato and Cicero? Why are they important? And what have they to do with us today?

The answer to the first question is uncontroversial. They were Greek Philosophers, who predated St Augustine, St Paul and Jesus. Plato by about 300 years and Cicero by about 100. Both are still studied today.

Their importance is that they helped form the intellectual climate in Biblical times, in much the same way as the thoughts of Charles Darwin, Adam Smith, Karl Marx *et al* do today.

Furthermore, most of the New Testament was written in Greek and St Paul, in particular, would have studied their written works. In a number of places this Greek philosophical influence can be detected in his letters, and indeed in some of the gospels.

But why does this matter to us? I offer two reasons. The first is rather technical, and concerns the way we understand and use the Bible – particularly the difficult bits. These difficult bits often have their roots in cultural and language differences, rather than in the truths the words express. So, difficulty does not mean we should throw our arms up in despair and abandon our Bible reading, but rather make use of the many aids available to us – from the simplicity of daily Bible reading notes to more substantial Bible commentaries and concordances to de-fuddle[1] the difficulties.

The second reason lies in what St Augustine is saying in this quote. He is well aware that many influential thinkers have wise and wonderful things to say. But he compares them with this one invitation of Jesus, found in Matthew 11:28 (KJV).

> "Come unto me, all ye that labour and are heavy laden, and I will give you rest."

It stands in stark contrast to the sayings of Plato and Cicero – and, indeed, to any of the sayings of any other major thinker in any age, simply because it marks a   personal claim by Jesus of what He is able to do if people would only come to Him and accept His help.

Putting it another way, clever and wise thoughts can be useful but are not enough. Although St Augustine doesn't spell it out fully here, the Christian claim is that only through relationship with Jesus can a person become empowered to live out the ethics found in, for example, the Sermon on the Mount.

In effect St Augustine is making a claim for the uniqueness and superiority of Christ over all others, a claim that mainstream Christianity still makes today.

---

[1] For more on this see the author's *De-Fuddling the Bible*; details on page ***

Thou hast created us
for thyself
and our heart is not quiet
unless it rests in thee.

St. Augustine: Article 13

Thou hast created us for thyself and our heart is not quiet unless it rests in thee.

This quotation from St Augustine answers questions concerning the meaning, purpose and point of life.

People have worried about this throughout history and still do so today. Then, as now, the questions would often be seen as too challenging, often ignored and pushed to the back of the mind. Occasionally some people would boldly assert that, in fact, there is no meaning or purpose to life, a philosophical position known as nihilism.

A nihilistic response to these questions can lead to depression, and even suicide, especially if the person troubled by such thoughts questions the point of continuing to live.

This leads naturally to the second part of the quote above, where St Augustine shares his own experience of reaching a place of calm and purpose in daily living. The heart was seen, in his day, as the seat of emotions rather than as a pump pushing the blood around the body as now. Consequently, calmness and quiet were seen as arising from a resting heart.

What then is the Christian position in this? The Bible asserts throughout that God is the creator of the whole universe, and that humankind is special. For me, this is what Genesis chapters 1 – 3 are all about. Rather than giving a blow-by-blow account of how things came into being, it tells us of the specialness of human beings in the world. It also tells us that things have gone wrong, and are not as God wished.

The rest of the Bible, for me, gives an account of how God has acted (and still acts) to put things right. First, through adopting a special nation and giving them commandments, as an example to everyone else of how humankind is meant to live, and how they can thereby have peace, joy and meaning in their lives. God's prophets and some of His actions in history reinforce this message.

But most importantly, when this approach was, at best, only partially successful, He came Himself in human form, as Jesus, with further teaching and demonstrated His love and concern for us through the Easter events. The invitation to us all to accept this, and accept the consequences and teaching around the Easter events, still stands.

I believe that this is what St Augustine was getting at, i.e. that this is the way in which our heart can be quietened and come to rest in Him.

Conclusion

Conclusion

St Augustine said much more of note than we have been able to consider in these short articles.

Opposite is a small selection that you might like to ponder.

Some are simple and straightforward to interpret and accept.

Others need considerable thought.

See how you get on.

Faith is to believe what you do not see; the reward of this faith is to see what you believe.	Indeed, man wishes to be happy even when he so lives as to make happiness impossible.
No saint is without a past And no sinner is without a future.	Chris is not valued at all Unless he is valued above all.
A thing is not necessarily true because it is badly uttered, nor false because spoken magnificently.	What does love look like? It has the hands to help others. It has the feet to hasten to the poor and needy. It has eyes to see misery and want. It has the ears to hear the sighs and sorrows of men. That is what love looks like.
Repentant tears wash out the stain of guilt.	The confession of evil works is the first beginning of good works.
God is not what you imagine or what you think you understand. If you understand Him, you have failed.	Lord take my heart from me, for I cannot give it to thee. Keep it for thyself, for I cannot keep it for thee; and save me in spite of myself.
It was pride that changed angels into devils; it is humility that makes men as angels.	Habit, if not resisted, soon becomes necessity.

If you have enjoyed these articles ...

... you may care to read the following two books which contain articles by Michael Penny on commonly held statements and questions as to whether they are true of false.

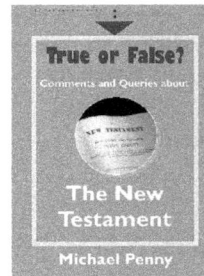

True or False? Comments and Queries about Christianity?
True or False? Comments and Queries about The New Testament?

- People need faith to be healed
- The Kingdom of God is within you
- The Kingdom is extended by kindness
- Pentecost is the *birthday* of the Church
- Confession is a 'must' for forgiveness
- Whoever is born of God does not sin
- Sexual morals are out of date
- We should do what Jesus would do
- The New Covenant belongs to Gentiles
- Prayer is a weapon
- Women should not teach men

Each of these two books by Michael Penny contain over thirty such comments and queries each. These are discussed in a thought-provoking manner for the aim of the books is to encourage people to 'think' about what they hear and read, and about what they believe. For example … Which of the above comments are true? And which are false?

Ideal for discussion subjects in home groups or for personal meditation.

These books are available as eBooks from Amazon and Apple and as paperbacks from Amazon.

They can also be ordered from www.obt.org.uk and from the publisher

The Open Bible Trust
Fiordland Mount, Upper Basildon,
Reading, RG8 8LU, UK.

De-fuddling the Bible

By Colin Smith

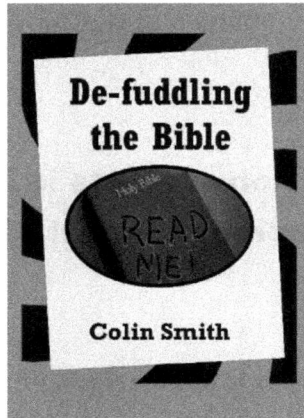

Christians have always found the Bible to be both an uplifting and intriguing book. Uplifting since its contents form the basis of their faith, and because it often "speaks" wisely into their current situation.

Yet it can also appear puzzling, confusing and muddled. Whilst this can be worrying and uncomfortable, it is the author's belief that this is normal, for it is through the struggle to make sense of it that we learn and grow.

This book aims to give the reader an insight into some of the causes of confusion, rather than to give solutions to specific problems. Once identified, and applied to a particular passage, many of the problems fall away and faith is reinforced. This process is the "de-fuddling" in the title.

It will be useful to all serious readers of the Bible, but perhaps especially so to Christians working alone, such as prisoners alone in their cell, members of the armed forces on deployment, and boarding school pupils alone in their dorm.

Copies of this book are available as eBooks from Amazon and Apple
and as paperbacks from Amazon.

They can also be ordered from www.obt.org.uk and from the publisher

The Open Bible Trust
Fiordland Mount, Upper Basildon,
Reading, RG8 8LU, UK.

About the author

Colin Smith is a retired Methodist Local preacher who lives in the High Peak of Derbyshire. His 25 years of preaching was mainly, but not entirely, within the loving intimacy of small, rural congregations. Throughout his Christian life he has regularly led and attended house groups and conferences. He has authored two other books, and a number of articles for Christian magazines.

He was educated at Swanwick Hall Grammar school in Derbyshire before attending Keele University in Staffordshire. Colin graduated, with a BA (hons) in Physics and Philosophy, and a Diploma in education. Although Physics was his "bread and butter" subject, he retained an interest in philosophy, particularly philosophical theology and apologetics.

After Keele, Colin spent six years as a science teacher in a church secondary school in Tororo, Uganda, during which time he married Irene. After a short spell teaching in the UK, he entered teacher education before finally becoming a Senior Lecturer at the Manchester Metropolitan University. During this time he gained a Masters degree from the University of Salford. He has also had part time roles of tutor, tutor counsellor and assistant lecturer for the Open University.

Following his recent retirement, Colin is spending time doing a little writing - and enjoying growing vegetables. Colin and Irene have two sons, and two lovely granddaughters.

Publications of The Open Bible Trust must be in accordance with its evangelical, fundamental and dispensational basis. However, beyond this minimum, writers are free to express whatever beliefs they may have as their own understanding, provided that the aim in so doing is to further the object of The Open Bible Trust. A copy of the doctrinal basis is available on **www.obt.org.uk** or from:

THE OPEN BIBLE TRUST
Fordland Mount, Upper Basildon,
Reading, RG8 8LU, UK

www.ingramcontent.com/pod-product-compliance
Lightning Source LLC
Chambersburg PA
CBHW060709030426
42337CB00017B/2810